W9-BCX-385

Doomed!

THE DONNER PARTY

By Kristen Rajczak

Gareth Stevens
PUBLISHING

Please visit our website, www.garethstevens.com. For a free color catalog
of all our high-quality books, call toll free 1-800-542-2595 or fax 1-877-542-2596.

Library of Congress Cataloging-in-Publication Data

Rajczak, Kristen.
 The Donner Party / Kristen Rajczak.
    pages cm. — (Doomed!)
 Includes bibliographical references and index.
 ISBN 978-1-4824-2928-2 (pbk.)
 ISBN 978-1-4824-2929-9 (6 pack)
 ISBN 978-1-4824-2930-5 (library binding)
 1. Donner Party—Juvenile literature. 2. Pioneers—California—History—19th century—
Juvenile literature. 3. Pioneers—West (U.S.)—History—19th century—Juvenile literature. 4.
Overland journeys to the Pacific—Juvenile literature. 5. Frontier and pioneer life—West
(U.S.)—Juvenile literature. 6. Sierra Nevada (Calif. and Nev.)—History—19th century—
Juvenile literature. I. Title.
 F868.N5R35 2015
 978'.02—dc23

                                    2014048076

First Edition

Published in 2016 by
Gareth Stevens Publishing
111 East 14th Street, Suite 349
New York, NY 10003

Designer: Katelyn E. Reynolds
Editor: Therese Shea

Photo credits: Cover, p. 1 Fotosearch/Getty Images; cover, pp. 1–32 (background
texture) 501room/Shutterstock.com; p. 5 De Agostini Picture Library/Getty Images; p. 7
The United States government/Wikipedia.org; p. 9 Ann Ronan Pictures/Print Collector/
Getty Images; p. 10 Lansford Hastings/Wikipedia.org; p. 11 Kean Collection/Archive
Photos/Getty Images; p. 13 Hamik/Shutterstock.com; p. 14 Reproduced from his book:
The Emigrants' Guide to Oregon and California; George Conclin, publisher; Cincinnati,
Ohio/Wikipedia.org; p. 15 Mitch Johanson/Shutterstock.com; p. 17 Phil Schermeister/
National Geographic/Getty Images; p. 19 Moni3/Wikipedia.org; p. 21 Carmel Studios/
SuperStock/Getty Images; p. 23 T. H. O'Sullivan of the U.S. Geological Exploration of
the Fortieth Parallel (King Survey)/Wikipedia.org; p. 24 Online Archive of California/
Wikipedia.org; p. 25 Joseph Warren Revere/Wikipedia.org; p. 27 (diary page) Patrick
Breen wrote the page/Wikipedia.org; p. 27 (James and Margaret Reed) Ethan Rarick's
book, *Desperate Passages*, published by Oxford University Press, 2008/Wikipedia.org;
p. 29 Universal History Archive/Getty Images.

Printed in the United States of America

CPSIA compliance information: Batch #CS15GS: For further information contact Gareth Stevens, New York, New York at 1-800-542-2595.

CONTENTS

Words in the glossary appear in **bold** type
the first time they are used in the text.

MISFORTUNE IN THE MOUNTAINS

In late 1846, a group of **emigrants** were trapped high in the mountains of the Sierra Nevada. Heading for California, the wagon train had taken an untried shortcut that proved to be far more challenging than the established route. Now, snowdrifts surrounded their shelters, and food supplies were low. Even if someone was looking for them, the snow was so high and the wind so strong, it seemed unlikely their camp could be reached—or that they'd live much longer in the cold conditions.

Many in the group, called the Donner party, believed they were doomed. Nonetheless, of the nearly 90 men, women, and children stranded in the high mountain pass, about half survived. How they stayed alive remains one of the most **gruesome** stories in US history: Some said they ate their dead!

The Deadly Details

In 1844, James K. Polk was elected US president. He was in favor of the nation expanding, and groups like the Donner party heading west to settle.

This illustration shows what one artist thought a group of emigrants might have looked like while traveling through the Rocky Mountains. Native Americans look on.

EYEWITNESSES

Historians and others who have studied the Donner party know a lot about what happened because of primary sources. A primary source is a **document** such as a letter or item such as a plate that can tell us about the time period it was created. Members of the Donner party wrote diaries and letters about their experiences. These accounts can be used to figure out how and when the events occurred.

5

A DECADE OF EXPANSION

The year the Donner party set out was important in the history of US expansion. In 1846, both Oregon and Texas became US states. That year, President Polk also declared war with Mexico, which resulted in the addition of California, New Mexico, Nevada, Arizona, Utah, and parts of Wyoming and Colorado 2 years later. The 1840s were a decade **dedicated** to expanding the United States from coast to coast.

The lure of all this land was strong for many. Those in government believed they'd increase trade with Asia by having ports on the West Coast. Thousands of families were heading west at the start of the 1840s, hearing there was good, plentiful land. Businesses followed with the goal of supplying the populations moving to the new territories.

The Deadly Details

Between 1846 and 1850, the United States gained 1.2 million square miles (3.1 million sq km) of new land.

By 1840, more than 7 million Americans lived beyond the Appalachian Mountains on the "frontier." As more territory was added to the United States, the frontier got bigger and bigger for pioneers wishing to settle there.

Oregon Territory
1846

Louisiana Purchase
1803

Spanish Cession
1819

Mexican Cession
1848

Gadsden Purchase
1853

Texas Annexation
1845

MANIFEST DESTINY

A newspaper writer named John O'Sullivan coined a phrase in 1845 to describe the reason Americans were being drawn to the West: manifest destiny. He was writing in favor of adding Texas as a state, but his words came to influence overall expansion. O'Sullivan wrote that Americans were destined, or fated, to spread across North America and govern it. Both those in government and emigrants embraced the idea.

STARTING OUT

In the spring of 1846, George Donner put an ad in a Springfield, Illinois, newspaper. He was looking for a few young men to help him lead a team of oxen to California, where he was going to settle with his family. Families who wanted to join Donner's party and head out for California answered the ad, too.

Donner was a farmer bringing along his wife, Tamsen, and five daughters. His brother Jacob, Jacob's wife Elizabeth, and their seven children were also traveling with them. The Donners joined with a group led by James Reed that included Reed's wife, mother-in-law, four children, and others.

The group arrived in Independence, Missouri, a common starting point for pioneers heading west, on May 10, 1846.

The Deadly Details

The Reeds were easy to spot in the wagon train. Their wagon had two levels and was called the "palace car." It was a burden along the way, however, as it was heavy to pull and hard to get over rough **terrain**.

The journey by wagon to California was supposed to take 4 to 6 months. Many pioneers traveled west on foot while the wagons carried their belongings.

A HARD ROAD

Both George Donner and James Reed moved around a lot during their lives, so the trip to California wasn't a scary new beginning for them. For many pioneers, though, heading west was a big risk. They left behind family, friends, and homes for a place they'd never seen before. They also had to leave behind furniture and family **heirlooms**. The wagons could only hold so much, and food for the journey was the most important cargo.

9

The group from Springfield bought more needed supplies in Independence and likely added a few more wagons to their party. They then crossed the plains without any problems and arrived at Fort Laramie, Wyoming, at the beginning of July.

It was around this time that Donner and Reed's desire to follow a route different from the established California Trail began to be discussed. A man named Lansford Hastings had written a book called *The Emigrants' Guide to Oregon and California*. Hastings claimed there was a way to cut several hundred miles off the long route to California (though he had never traveled it himself). In addition, he offered to lead any group on this shortcut should they meet him at Fort Bridger, Wyoming.

ThE DEadLy DEtaiLS

The Donner party was hoping to reach the Sacramento Valley in California.

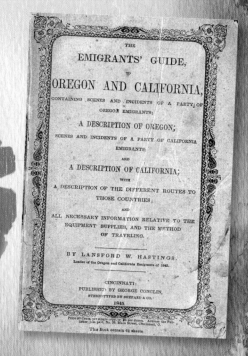

THE
EMIGRANTS' GUIDE,
TO
OREGON AND CALIFORNIA,
CONTAINING SCENES AND INCIDENTS OF A PARTY OF
OREGON EMIGRANTS;
A DESCRIPTION OF OREGON;
SCENES AND INCIDENTS OF A PARTY OF CALIFORNIA
EMIGRANTS;
AND
A DESCRIPTION OF CALIFORNIA;
WITH
A DESCRIPTION OF THE DIFFERENT ROUTES TO
THOSE COUNTRIES;
AND
ALL NECESSARY INFORMATION RELATIVE TO THE
EQUIPMENT, SUPPLIES, AND THE METHOD
OF TRAVELING.

BY LANSFORD W. HASTINGS,
Leader of the Oregon and California Emigrants of 1842.

CINCINNATI:
PUBLISHED BY GEORGE CONCLIN,
STEREOTYPED BY SHEPARD & CO.
1845.

Price 50 Cents, per single Copy. ... $4 per dozen. Address the Pub-
lisher, post paid, No. 25, Main Street, Cincinnati, O.
This Book contains 3½ sheets.

As its name suggests, the Oregon Trail led emigrants northwest to the area near present-day Portland, Oregon.

CALIFORNIA TRAIL

The Donner party began their journey on what's now called the California Trail. This route crossed the western half of the modern-day United States, beginning in several places in Missouri and reaching a few parts of California. Much of the trail followed the famous Oregon Trail over the Rocky Mountains, but then headed southwest across present-day Utah. More than 250,000 emigrants used this route to reach California during the 1840s and 1850s.

HASTINGS CUTOFF

Along the way, the group met a messenger on horseback carrying a letter to anyone traveling that road. It was from Lansford Hastings! The letter encouraged them to keep going and wait for him at Fort Bridger. This gave Donner and Reed hope that they were making the right decision in following Hastings.

Some of the group weren't interested in following the untested "Hastings Cutoff" route. They'd stay on the same path for some time before continuing on to the known trail. Meanwhile, nearly 90 people, including George Donner and James Reed, arrived in Fort Bridger, Wyoming, almost 2 weeks after getting Hastings' letter. Hastings wasn't there.

George Donner was chosen as the leader of the group. He had to decide what to do next.

The Deadly Details

James Reed met a friend from Springfield while at Fort Laramie, a man familiar with the terrain of the shortcut. He warned Reed against traveling the Hastings Cutoff. Reed didn't listen.

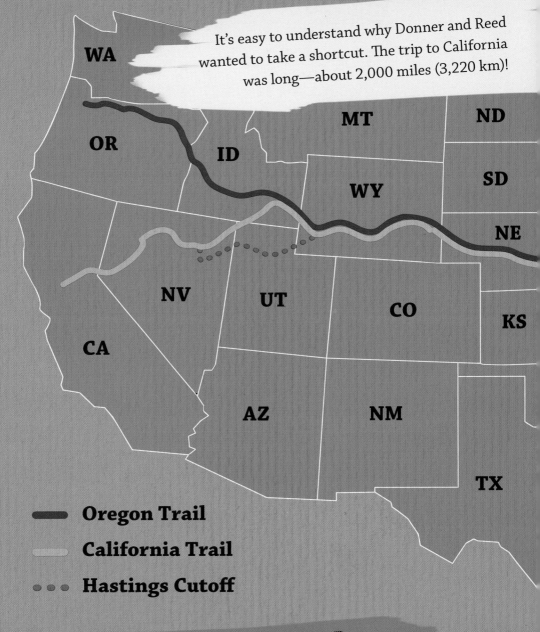

It's easy to understand why Donner and Reed wanted to take a shortcut. The trip to California was long—about 2,000 miles (3,220 km)!

WA
OR
ID
MT
ND
SD
WY
NE
NV
UT
CO
KS
CA
AZ
NM
TX

━━━ **Oregon Trail**

━━━ **California Trail**

●●● **Hastings Cutoff**

WHO WAS HASTINGS?

Lansford Hastings was a lawyer from Ohio, but he spent the early 1840s traveling around the Oregon and California Territories. He began a land development business in northern California with a man named John Sutter. In order to be a success, though, the pair needed emigrants to make the journey to their land. In 1845, Hastings published his guide for those wanting to travel west, including the cutoff as a way to reach California.

13

Hastings had already left the fort to lead another wagon train. He left word that the Donner party should follow him, and he would mark the trail as he went. The party stayed at the fort a few days to rest and followed Hastings' directions.

On August 6, they reached a canyon. Hastings had stuck a note on a bush there saying the trail was hard, but he would come help them soon. They waited days for Hastings to return. Finally, Reed rode ahead to find him. He did, but Hastings said he wouldn't come back. He pointed out a new way, which turned out to be even more difficult. The party wasted almost 2 weeks cutting a path through the trees and brush.

The Deadly Details

The path cut by the Donner party through the Wasatch Mountains was used for a decade after they passed through it.

Lansford Hastings

The Hastings Cutoff took the Donner party through the Wasatch Mountains, a very difficult route for wagons.

FORTS ON THE FRONTIER

Forts were built on the American frontier as far back as the American Revolution. They served as places for settlers to hide during war or attacks from Native American tribes. Fort Laramie was first built in 1834 as a private fur trading post. Fort Bridger was originally built in the 1840s as a place for emigrants to stop for supplies on the Oregon Trail. Having these forts along the trails was critical to emigrants' survival.

CHALLENGES CONTINUE

Crossing the Wasatch Mountains was especially hard on the animals in the Donner party. The oxen were exhausted when the group walked out of the mountain range toward the end of August. However, the worst part of the journey was about to begin. At the foot of the Wasatch Mountains in present-day Utah is the Great Salt Lake Desert. While the party brought what water they could, it wasn't enough to take them across it. The Reed family lost its oxen, and many wagons had to be abandoned.

It took 5 days to cross the desert. Once across, the party discovered their supplies wouldn't be enough to get them to California. A few men rode out ahead for their **destination**, promising to bring relief when they could.

The DeadLy DetaiLS

At the end of September, the Donner party reached the Humboldt River and rejoined the California Trail. The cutoff had *added* 125 miles (201 km) to their journey!

The Great Salt Lake Desert receives fewer than 5 inches (13 cm) of **precipitation** each year. It's not a good idea to cross without a lot of water, as the Donner party found out.

BANISHED

The difficulty of the journey was wearing on the Donner party. On October 5, Reed's wagon got tangled with that of another family. The driver of that wagon, John Snyder, began hitting the oxen with his whip. Reed tried to stop him, but got hit instead. Angry, Reed pulled out a knife and stabbed Snyder, who died from the wound. Though some wanted Reed killed, he was **banished** instead. He rode off, leaving his family behind.

17

WINTER HITS

The Donner party arrived at the Sierra Nevada in mid-October, weeks later than they planned. They knew it was only a matter of time before the snow would start to fall in the high mountains. One of the men who had ridden ahead rejoined the group around October 19 with supplies and two Native American guides. The party's joy at this was soon dashed as the first blizzard of the season hit days later. It blocked the mountain passes.

The Donner brothers and their families had fallen behind the rest of the group. They were able to put up a few tents before the snow got too bad. Others made it as far as Truckee Lake, where they sheltered in one cabin and quickly built a few more.

The Deadly Details

The Donner brothers' group numbered about 22. They were on Alder Creek about 6 miles (10 km) away from the larger group.

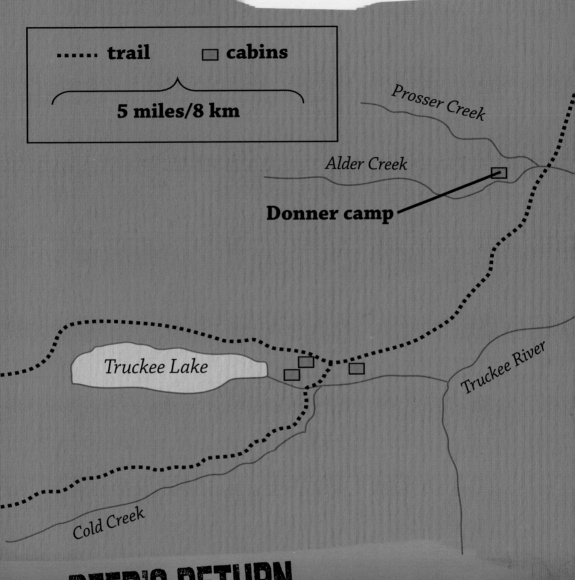

Families crowded into small cabins near Truckee Lake, now called Donner Lake.

..... trail   ☐ cabins

5 miles/8 km

Prosser Creek

Alder Creek

Donner camp

Truckee Lake

Truckee River

Cold Creek

REED'S RETURN

The banished James Reed arrived at Sutter's Fort in the Sacramento Valley in bad shape. He knew his family and the rest of the Donner party would be, too. He packed supplies and headed back to the mountains, with the hope of saving his family. Reed couldn't make it through the snow and returned to the fort to ask for help. However, most men there had left to fight the war with Mexico.

19

LIFE IN THE MOUNTAINS

The winter the Donner party spent in the Sierra Nevada was one of the worst winters that area had ever seen. It was cold, and the snow fell heavy and often. Those at Alder Creek were especially cold in their tents built of branches, quilts, and coats. They tried to light fires, but sometimes went without a fire for days.

Food was scarce. The group ate the animals brought with them—even family dogs. They trapped mice and wild animals when they could, but the meat was never enough, so they burned the bones and ate those, too.

Several members of the Donner party had already died on the way to the Sierra Nevada. However, starvation and freezing temperatures took the lives of many more.

The Deadly Details

The Donner party was stranded only about 150 miles (241 km) from Sutter's Fort.

Today, visitors can hike the Donner Camp Trail at Alder Creek—but it's a good idea to avoid going in the winter!

THE WASHOE

A group of Native Americans called the Washoe lived near where the emigrants were stranded. During the harsh winters in the mountains, they moved to lower elevations. They stored food they had gathered and hunted earlier in the year. However, some would wear snowshoes to go out hunting or fishing. Washoe **oral history** says some Washoe gave the Donner party rabbit and potatoes, but were shot at when bringing the camp a deer!

21

RESCUE

The Donner party hoped the weather would warm enough at some point to get them over the mountains. It didn't. In mid-December, a small group left with a little food and handmade snowshoes to find help. They got lost in the mountains. This was the first group said to resort to cannibalism for survival. Some of them reached a house at the bottom of the Sierra Nevada about a month later and asked for help. A relief party was sent out.

Meanwhile, men were returning to Sutter's Fort from the war with Mexico. Reed gathered some help and finally headed back into the mountains to find his family and the rest of the Donner party.

The first rescue party reached Truckee Lake on February 19. The camp seemed empty, but they finally found the starving survivors.

The DeadLy DetaiLS

Archaeologists found that members of the Donner party ate "glue," or boiled animal hides.

Donner Pass is found at an elevation of about 7,000 feet (2,130 m).

DONNER PASS

The mountain pass where the Donner party wintered in 1846 and 1847 has been named for them, the Donner Pass. Today, the pass is one of the main routes connecting San Francisco, California, and Reno, Nevada. It's found within Tahoe National Forest near a park also named for the Donner party—Donner Memorial State Park. And the pass is still known for very snowy winters, including an 8-day blizzard that hit in 1952!

The first relief party was unable to help all the starving travelers back to Sutter's Fort. They took about two dozen and left the rest of the group with a little food, though it still wasn't much. Reed's rescue party reached the Donner party soon after. Reed was reunited with his wife and children, whom he had feared were dead.

Over the course of about 2 months, groups traveled back and forth between Sutter's Fort in California and the camps on Truckee Lake and Alder Creek. However, of those who waited for help, many died. In addition, the rescue parties were hit with more snow, making their journeys back to Sutter's Fort difficult, especially with sick people in tow.

The Deadly Details

Many accounts of cannibalism at Truckee Lake and Alder Creek were said to have happened in the weeks between relief parties.

John Sutter

John Sutter, the same man Lansford Hastings worked with, built Sutter's Fort. He was helpful to Reed in supplying the rescue party.

SAFE AND SOUND

The members of the Donner party who survived all made it to Sutter's Fort by late April 1847. Their return was big news in California—especially their possible cannibalism. Upon the finding of the lost emigrants, the *California Star* had reported: "I could state several most horrid circumstances connected with this affair: such as one of the women being **obliged** to eat part of the body of her father and brother, another saw her husband's heart cooked."

CANNIBALS?

Until recently, the Donner party was famous for becoming desperate and eating their companions' remains. Survivors of the ordeal said there was cannibalism. Letters and journals written by the Donner party also say this. Even Washoe oral history states that the party was seen eating human remains.

However, no physical proof has yet been found! For many years, this was because archaeologists didn't know for sure where the Donner camp was. Around 2002, an archaeologist and her team seemed to uncover the Alder Creek camp. They unearthed plates, the remains of the party's fire, and thousands of tiny pieces of bone. Because of the story of cannibalism, these were of particular interest. Some of the bones studied were cow, deer, and rabbit.

The Deadly Details

Some bone pieces couldn't be identified because they had been cooked, likely for the party to eat.

James and Margaret Reed

CAN'T RULE IT OUT

Even though there's no physical proof yet, archaeologists can't say there wasn't any cannibalism at Alder Creek, Truckee Lake, or among the rescue party. First of all, there are the accounts of survivors. What an unpleasant lie they would have been telling! Second, it's possible that bones haven't been found or that the group only ate the soft parts of their companions and the rest has rotted away. There's also the matter of the bone pieces that couldn't be identified. They could be human!

27

BEGINNING LIFE IN CALIFORNIA

Surviving members of the doomed Donner party went on to own businesses, get married, and live long lives. But many Americans had heard the horrible tale of the Donner party. Some would-be settlers likely decided not to take on the difficult journey because of the story.

Then gold was found in California in 1848. A flood of pioneers—called the gold rush—went west to try their hand at finding a fortune. Fear of a fate like the Donner party was replaced by the promise of wealth at the end of the terrible mountain route. Still, the story of the Donner party has become part of the great story of US expansion. Whether that tale includes cannibalism may never be completely certain.

The Deadly Details

One Donner party survivor may have made a fortune during the gold rush!

28

While the troubles of the Donner party may have given some emigrants pause, the country continued to expand to become the nation that today stretches from sea to shining sea.

CALIFORNIA'S STATEHOOD

Following the discovery of gold, the population of nonnatives in California grew from about 1,000 to 100,000 in a few years! This made the territory a large addition to the country when it became a US state in 1850. Around Sutter's Fort grew the city of Sacramento, first as a miners' trading center. It later became the state's capital. The gold rush also encouraged the growth of many other California cities, such as San Francisco.

29

GLOSSARY

banish: to drive out

dedicate: to commit to a goal

destination: the place to which somebody or something is going

document: a formal piece of writing

emigrant: someone who leaves his or her native land to live in another country or territory

gruesome: causing horror or disgust

heirloom: something handed down through a family over many years

obliged: forced

oral history: stories passed down by word of mouth

precipitation: rain, snow, sleet, or hail

terrain: the type of land in an area

FOR MORE INFORMATION

BOOKS

Hale, Nathan. *Donner Dinner Party*. New York, NY: Amulet Books, 2013.

Huey, Lois Miner. *American Archaeology Uncovers the Westward Movement*. New York, NY: Marshall Cavendish Benchmark, 2010.

Schwartz, Heather E. *The Foul, Filthy American Frontier: The Disgusting Details About the Journey Out West*. Mankato, MN: Capstone Press, 2010.

WEBSITES

Donner Party
www.history.com/topics/donner-party
Watch a video and read more about the Donner party.

Map of the Donner Party Route
www.pbs.org/wgbh/americanexperience/features/map-widget/donner-map/
Check out this interactive map showing how the Donner party traveled west.

Westward Expansion Timeline
www.ducksters.com/history/westward_expansion/timeline.php
Learn more about the time period of the Donner party by using this timeline.

INDEX